Beware Doomsday Fantasy

Or, The Systemic Persecution of the Individual

Or, How I Learned to Never Ask My Landlord to Fix My Air Conditioning

Sandy Press

Beware the Bourgeois Doomsday Fantasy

by Heath Brougher

Copyright © 2024 Heath Brougher

All rights reserved

Cover design, cover preparation, artwork
& interior layout
by harry k stammer

ISBN: 979-8-9898666-8-7
Printed in U.S.A.

Sandy Press
Queensland, Australia
&
California, USA

https://sandy-press.com
sandypress2021@gmail.com

"To me, authority is something that a freer spirit, a more independent mind, and a person who can handle the world, doesn't need guidance from."

—-George Carlin

*****__Warning:__ I live in fear for my life in Shit Towne aka York, PA. Every time I leave my apartment, I feel a palpable aura wrought by the regionail police who have already attempted to kill me once and are constantly profiling and harassing me. I've even been approached by a cop with a "what are you up to?" attitude while sitting on a bench reading a book—*five times!* in one year! (2023). This book is my way of protecting myself. This warning is a dire reveille built of words in case I am ever killed by a regional police officer—or any police officer in case they outsource the killing. If so, I need _everyone_ who reads this book to keep as much light and attention on that particular officer as possible because they are a **__murderer__**! I am a Pacifist and would never kill anyone. I have continuously had my civil rights violated by the regional police and it seems to get worse by the day. From profiling me to destroying the cartilage in both of my knees, these are dangerous and deadly officers. Why do they hate me? They do not understand me. I have long hair and a beard That, mixed with my tendency to live free instead of purveying the pablum that freedom is found within a flag. So, please, if one of them kills me—*__keep the light on them!__* Hold them accountable! Show them they cannot kill at will! Show them that speaking your "rude Truths" and cultivating your intellect and simply looking different than the intolerant sheepfold, is *not* a crime! Show the police True Freedom—no matter how much it scares them! Show the police how to do the right thing! Today, they are coming after me. Who knows? Tomorrow, it could be *you* as the globe slips into the vile cracks of fascism!*****

Beware the Bourgeois Doomsday Fantasy

by Heath Brougher

Sandy Press

Gist

Retrain the regionail police! Did you know the powers that be might try to kill you if you look "different" in their limited rote-thought patters eternally stuck in a negative feedback loop? It's true. Found it out the hard way. Like this. After helping Black Lives Matter and having the audacity to have long hair and a beard along with a tendency to engage in freedom and creativity, the regionail police had no choice. It was a foregone conclusion they bring their corrupt profiling fugazi of authority into my life as I was mourning my mother's death. Officer Criminal and Judge Liar spake falsehoods unto me repeatedly. I cannot leave my apt without being harassed. Who the hell gets "in trouble" 5 times in one year for sitting on a bench and reading a fuckin' book? The answer—me, the wielder of Truth—the one who scares the police shitless while also serving as their official punching bag since these regionails are a product of abstractions and live to perpetuate the pablum of the post-postmodern and enforce the extremely dangerous and inherently insane societal abstractions they were birthed from.

The regional police took my cartilage,

so I will take off the masks they wicked-wear

and expose them to the world.

Gimcrack

The day white people invented stealing was the first of this long-drawn-out trek to Humanity's inevitable end. Humans will have a blast and then give a mightily muddled planet back to its millions of rightful owners—and only several millennia too late! Do rightwing wrongs make a wrongwing right? Is there a balance hereabouts, even if nonsensical, that has never been pondered before? Unsure usurper. I'll have another bowl of strawberryspeckled tablecloth along with my seventh bowl of smashed potatoes as we picnic on a sundrenched day at Potter's Field.
The police do not live to protect and serve.
They live to harass and maim.

Gimp

After an unknown undercover regional police officer stole the cartilage from my knees, I, obviously, had to heal from the wounds they grifted me. This took form in my going on a daily "gimpwalk" which is dangerous because I have to go out among the jaded soullessness of not just the regionail police but the people they herd and hurt.
I *will not* let them bring me down.

Gnarl

You are tantamount to the chaos and killing that occurs in spontaneous riots. You feast upon your brothers and sisters. You cause the summers to end early. You rust out the silver linings. You have never raised the bells. You have only brightened the blight. You are jargon and rotgut. You are racism and radiated rats. You are searingly superfluous and continuously cough your copish craziness into the world. Your existence makes the human-experience a darker place.

I am the one whose head you will bash open.

.

Goo

The regional police = a vessel of dark fairytstories and brutal action architectured to control the masses and spill forth a narrative of rote smokestacken ideologies bearing the *lean* of Mussolini. Their voice is the frequency of violence and phoniness, vibrating without even trying to guise their blatant wavelength of lies and hypocrisies—spewing venom upon the overbroken cattle as they are the Gordon Prichards and Robert Barrons run amuck the great bait ball of 'merican society. It echoes through the corridors of consciousness and overall essence of a coldblooded Pennsylvanianistic pedantry—

A monochromatic monotone kaleidoscope
of words
of worlds parsed
of decency,
of symphony.
Instead, eyes of euthanized Estonias
of no mercy,
of starving eggless India.
Their eyes, yes, glimmering in an empty glimpse
of soulless frightening—
causing Sanity to be under constant siege
as they wait to escort me to a genocidal ambulance.

Eyes that have endured the removal
of integrity, vulnerability, magnanimity.
Eyes insanitized and Pavlovianly perpetuating
the pain of state sponsored brutality and gimpage
are the eyes that have fixed their gaze upon me.

Grift

The police have polyester hearts and polyethylene souls and are not afraid to show it. They live with a violent certainty placed into the densest vagueness of a world they could never fully understand. They are the keepers of the Quo, the representatives of the Rote. They see in black and white and try to destroy anyone who does not fold and bend and blend in with the paisley white sheepfold as they tote around their Totalitary mindset and know, deep down inside, they are the O.G.s—the "original gangstas."

Gloom

A cop should be
washed of ego;

a cop should be
exorcised of hatred;
instead these evil lawmen live
to binge on these two toxic
and rampant societal insanities;

a cop should have
at least a rough-shod idea
of integrity and mercy;

instead, they live in a decency-parched
limbo, obliviously taking orders
from the wealthy elite—who have always
been their real employers
and the only people they will Truly protect.

Ghats (thanks to Will Alexander for this title which I read in his book *The Combustion Cycle*, meaning "where Hindus burn their dead")

The sheepy policeyfold drags ass with a severe case of *schismwarts acquired after years of syphilis kisses. This fault lies with the corrupt climate and politicians and *you!* Yes, Jonny Q Po, regionail officer, *you* are responsible for the death of decency and the rise of fascism and racism that struck society quick and ruthless as an errant idiotic wreckingball. You carry a totlitary mentality looked through as a rote-hewn reality perceiving the world through your blue and red bloodlights. I say to thee: AWAKEN UP! {pretend like I'm clapping my hands right in front of your face} AWAKEN UP! {don't get Woke} but AWAKEN UP! AWAKEN THE FUCK UP!
Awaken up you pathetically-pulsed American deathsuckers! AWAKEN UP! {now I'm nudging you!—the police and the sheepfold}
You are content to be fat and happy.
Why not be skinny and pissed!?
Ever thought about trying out that "thinkin thang" you've heard about your entire robotic and mandatorily mediocre lives? You allowed the demons to run amuck! In fact, you have become the demons run amuck! I wish I could show you some mercy but you showed me none and I only fight with the pen—not the militarized weapons you've armed yourself to the teeth with. You are "letting it happen" in the Orwellian sense.

I learned to live free—and this is why they want to kill me.

*look Heller, no shoelaces!

Grimace

I am the face void of mascara—
a maskless visage—
the reality behind the eminence front
of the profiling shroud of the enfolded sleepy peoplies.

For every
Truth I speak another bullet is loaded
into the gun that will cancel
my bruised and scar-hewn face.

I know, now, for certain, evil prevails—
that is… most of the time…

but not *this* time.

Guts

What else should I've expected
from a copied and pasted cop?—>
I must be growing more jaded
than I thought as I age—>

I didn't even touch the ball
but it was *you*, Officer Criminal,
who committed the flagrant foul.

Truth
will
out
and I will speak the word pristine.

Gnat

The dyslexic ineptitude
of these "law *en*-**FORCING**" Nazis!
I am Joseph K.
I am Public Enemy.
I was nailed to the pang-wracked crucifix of supra-profiling and left to suffer the nightmares of the hollowhearted injustice system. Another dogma having its day. Wrapped in the wicked robes of Io, Yeats' center collapsed ages ago.
We're left a nation without a collective
[or individual—*what does that word mean?*] clue.

Grit

Never in my life have I seen not only the police but the dead people, the members of the sleepy sheepfold, the existence-riddled nonexistent masses, *this* runnin' scared. If the regionail police violate my civil rights every chance they get—while also trying to, possibly, intimidate me with their constant presence, will someone please inform them that not only do I not scare easy, I actually don't scare *at all*. So, please feel free to tell every one of them that I do not fear their fuzzyheaded misinterpretation of me in the least. They can shoot me but they cannot kill me. Not in the abstract. I've got a zillion other massive creations I'd love to complete but I've already vastly surpassed my wildest dreams. If they empty a full clip into me {the cowardly and only way they know how to shoot a person} I would go to my grave with nothing but gratitude for the wonderful life this Multidimensional Multiverse has carved into its magnificent magnetic imprint for me.

.

Grandiloquent

I stomp my perpetual journey of gratitude. My gimpwalks are multitudinously epiphanic odes to the Multidimensional Multiverse as it communicates with me by the electric clacking at the top of my spine. I am the Boo Radley of Kingsgate Shopping Center——though I've grown ambivalent about whether or not I'll stick around till the end when everyone will need me to save them. I have Officer Criminal to thank for my realization of "why do I keep trying to help these slaves if all they ever do is put me down and spit in my face and try to kill me?" I've always been bit in the ass by my own integrity—which used to be considered a valiant trait, integrity, that is—along with individuality and self-actualization. Nowadays, not only are these traits not valued——they're looked down upon! This is what happens when the sleepy sheepies make a virtue of stupidity and the toxicity of the woke left and woke right are blind to what Wokery Truly is—> a guised fascism infiltrating their scared-to-death safe havens within the cozy "socially acceptable" crevices they've carved out for themselves with the other unexisters.

Grotesque

If by appearance alone the masses are afraid of you→
the genius of the crowd will quickly
flip on a full-throttled frenzy of hatred
and bring a callous conflagration
to burn away the genuine essence
of your uttering existence.
Anything different or unique
will be flayed by zealous sycophants of the Quo
in the phake belief this keeps us equal.

No one loves (hell, lives) to hate like 'mericans.
Especially 'merican regionail police.

Gavel

A stern gaze from the idiot king who thought he held authority over me, you, anybody. Nothin' worse than a judge! And that Judge Liar was as jaded and longlost from the intoxicant of imaginary power as they come. What does it say about someone when they wish to spend every day of their work-life doing nothing more than destroying the lives of other people for their insatiable "authority trip/dopamine hit" which I have never understood. I'd feel like a total jerk if I treated people the way an average judgecop treats people. Most of them have to be hurting deeply inside if they try to hide it by treating complete strangers like shit. And, on top of that, I don't even think they know the depths of their depression and unlived dreams is broadcast plain as day to the average member of the Quo.
What type of person do you have to be if you want to ruin people's lives all day long? What does it say about a person who throws people into cages for a living?

Ego mixed with insanity a dangerous Molotov cocktail makes. The horror of knowing the *last* place in the world you want to speak the Truth is in a court of law.

Guff

A 'merican courtroom is a place where the government beats up on its own constituents. Police are used to commit perjury. It's the unwritten duty they provide the State—the ever-abstracted State. It's the whole Pavlovianly-conditioned authority trip, as usual. Ain't nothing more dangerously insane than an american judge. Not only have they devoted their lives to enforcing the rampant social disease of insanity which proves to be nothing more than constructs of the Rote and ridiculous flights of imaginative fancy that were thought up by people who didn't know where the fuckin sun went at night. The ego of *any* judge is the size of Montana. Bigger. Not only are judges insane enough to believe in figments of imagination existing today as extremely dangerous societal illusions—but they have gone so far as to actually believe they, themselves, have/hold authority over another human being. This is not mentally healthy. This is due to the aforementioned severely-inflated ego. And they have the audacity to believe they can judge the sanity of another human being? Judges are perfect examples of insanity run amuck as a boxful of the world's dumbest pet rocks.

Git

with the program!

Don't forget→

This is ***America*** and you are *free*
   ... to do as you are told!

I repeat!

This is ***America*** and you are *free*
   ... to do as you are told!

Grace

Do the regionail police do the right thing? Maybe they help other people... "in theory." How often do you regionails actually help someone instead of preying and pounding on them to meet your bureaucratic quota? I know you turned me down 7 times when my life was threatened because it wasn't a "conditional threat." Well, that's one of the 7 different reasons for the lassitude and apathy I received every time I asked for your help. I know the real reason. Quite simple. You are heartless and flat out don't care if I live or die. Am I right or am I right? The regionails want to systematically route out the individual, the artist, the creative. If you step outta line by letting them see too much of your genius—which only subconsciously (and consciously) reminds them of their blatant shackles, they're gonna slap you around, if not take your life, out of frustration of their own weakness and falter phases and cages they live in without being cognizant.

Grail

I'm simply trying to be a good Christian, just like you regionail officers would want…right? Do the right thing? Help other people… how often do *you* regionails actually help someone instead of preying on them to meet your bureaucratic quota?
To quote the Holy Bible (first testament):

NAHUM : 3.5 and 3.6

"Behold, I am against you,
declares the lord of hosts,
and will lift up your skirts over your face;
and I will make nations look at your nakedness
and kingdoms at your shame.
I will cast abominable filth at you,
make you vile
and make you a spectacle."

Hey! I think that's the first time I've ever quoted the Quo's favorite dangerously insane book of science fiction. The unthinking majority love this book to death.

They took my cartilage—so I'll take their pride.

Gratitude

I do not have beliefs. For beliefs are dangerous. Beliefs allow the mind to stop functioning. A non-functioning mind is clinically dead. So, believe in *nothing.* I am barren of beliefs but I do have contentions—which is more than most humans can say. Most people find themselves either collapsing into the prerequisite behaviorisms and breastfed belief systems. But not me—at least I have my own unique contentions that exist outside the rote untrue crowd subconsciously moving toward Fascism and which will, inevitably, morph into a technocratic Oligarchy.

Grunt

Yes, the Truth can hurt. Just maybe these regionails will learn that because they don't understand someone doesn't make that person a "bad" (had to use a word they could understand) person. Maybe—just maybe, I can coax some vulnerability and empathy from out the regionail's heartlessness and birth a bit of nuanced tolerance to encroach on their current totalitarianism and overconfident rote-thought patterns. Isn't there a current pushback against bullies going on these days? Well, hopefully the police can be reproached for their bullying (and bludgeoning and attempted murder *and* murder). Maybe some of them will realize they're on the wrong side of the Dunning-Kruger effect.

Gargoyle

So, have I been too harsh? too abstract? too allovertheplace? too copkillin? too April showers? too imperfect? too ha ha ha? too flipscript? Well, your answer falls on deaf ears and no fears, Officer Criminal, and I don't give a fuck what you or anyone else thinks! Have I properly conveyed this sentiment? Don't you dare grin like the fuckin cop you are on the inside—and outside. You squawk the squawk of the beast. As KRS-One said "there can *never* really be justice on stolen land."

Grump

As so-called protectors of the insidious Quo, the regionail police are scared to death of the individual. They are more than well versed in free dumb but know nothing of Freedom. In fact, Freedom scares the half-alive shit out of them. This makes them extremely dangerous.

Hey, Mr. regionail policeman!

I know you're scared.

You should be.

For I come wielding the Truth.

"can't we all just get along?"

—Rodney King

Answer:

NO!→

the regionail police would never allow it!

Acknowledgements Page

Some writing published in "Beware the Bourgeois Doomsday Fantasy" has been previously published as part of other poems or essays in magazines such as *Cajun Mutt Press, Dissident Voice, Otoliths, Disturb The Universe Magazine, and Unlikely Stories.*

Made in the USA
Middletown, DE
09 January 2025